GW00992277

The Fun of the Fair

Contents

Trading fairs

Roman fairs

Fairs have been around for over 2500 years. Fairs began when Romans ruled the world.

Farmers took their goods to market. They took corn and cattle, hens and horses, goats and geese. But people wanted more than just the same old meat and bread and cheese and eggs. So once a year they had an extra market. A bigger market than all the rest, a fair. 'Fair' is an old Roman word for 'holiday'.

The Roman world

500 BC   0   500 AD

At a fair people could buy fine silk cloth from China and spices from India. Romans traded slaves for silk.

The Romans also had a fair for their god Bacchus. Bacchus was the Roman god of wine and fun. So Bacchus fairs were a time for Roman people to enjoy themselves. They lasted three days or more. The Romans watched plays, sang songs and ate a lot on their Bacchus holiday.

Roman fairs were mainly for trade but they were also a time for feasting and merry making.

Holy day fairs

In the Middle Ages, fairs in Europe were held on holy days.

Each saint had his (or her) own feast day, just as the Romans had a day for their Bacchus. Fairs were held on a saint's day so they were held outside the church.

St Audrey's Fair in Ely, in England, was held on St Audrey's Day.

St Bartholomew's Fair in London began on St Bartholomew's Day.

Did you know...

St Audrey's Fair sold a lot of cheap lace; anything cheap and tatty became known as 'St Audrey'. Today we use the word 'tawdry'.

Everyone went to the fair. No one worked on that day. The fair days were their holy days . . . or holidays.

Traders built wooden stalls. A stall was a table with a roof made from branches.

They sold goods and they also sold food. At those early European fairs there were sausages and roast pork, gingerbread and sugar plums for sale.

ges

airs

The Middle Ages

1000 AD   **New fairs begin in Europe**

1500 AD

2000 AD

5

In the Middle Ages people travelled
from all over the world to buy and sell
at fairs.

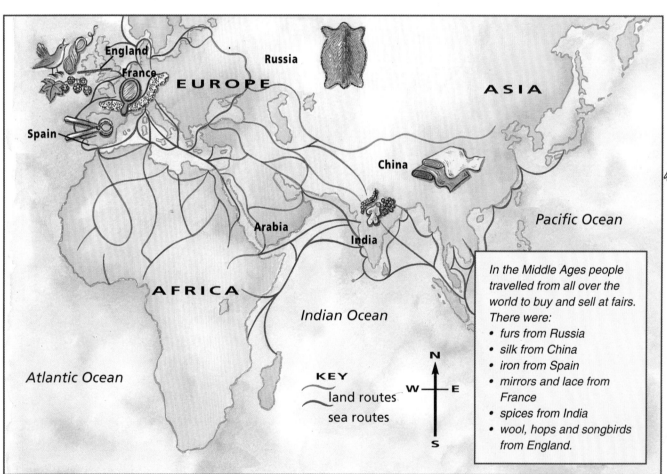

England
France
Russia
EUROPE
ASIA
Spain
China
Arabia
India
Pacific Ocean
AFRICA
Indian Ocean
Atlantic Ocean

KEY
land routes
sea routes

N
W — E
S

In the Middle Ages people
travelled from all over the
world to buy and sell at fairs.
There were:
• furs from Russia
• silk from China
• iron from Spain
• mirrors and lace from
  France
• spices from India
• wool, hops and songbirds
  from England.

The traders sold the goods they bought from each fair
at other markets and fairs around the world.

6

The Middle Ages

St Bartholomew's
Fair begins in
England 1133

Troyes Fair begins
in France
1150

1000

1100

120

The fairs in the Middle Ages were for fun as well as trading. At those fairs the people saw the colour and the mystery that they never saw the rest of the year. They could see . . .

people who sold wonder drinks . . .

juggling jesters . . .

magic-makers . . .

acrobats . . .

plays . . .

stilt walkers . . .

fire-eaters . . .

dancing bears.

Nizhni Novgorod
Fair begins in Russia
1250

1300

Stratford Mop Fair
begins in England
1350

1400

7

Frost fairs

By the end of the 1400s, the trading fairs were not so important. There were more ships carrying more goods. People could buy goods from another country at their own markets every week. They didn't have to wait for a yearly fair. But they still wanted fun and feasting so the fairs went on.

500 BC   *0*   *500 AD*

Did you know . . .

since 1564 the River Thames has frozen over nine times. The biggest Frost Fairs were held in 1608, 1684 and 1814.

Fairs were held everywhere. In 1608 the River Thames at London froze over. People held a fair upon the ice! Stalls were set up quickly. They made long streets across the river.

The ice was very thick. People lit fires on it and roasted meat. There were coach and horse races over the ice. People could play skittles or ride on swings in the middle of the River Thames.

In 1684 a Frost Fair on the Thames went on for five weeks. When the rain came down the stalls and tents began to float away!

Old London Bridge was pulled down in 1825. The new bridge let the river rush through. The ice could no longer form. The days of the Frost Fairs were over forever.

Food and fairings

People at fairs sold special food and presents for visitors to spend their money on. There was food like hot roasted meat, toffee apples, meat pies and gingerbread.

Fairs at Birmingham and Enfield sold nothing but gingerbread.

Did you know . . .

the pie-men usually sold mutton pies.

Simple Simon

Simple Simon met a pie-man, going to the fair;
Said Simple Simon to the pie-man,
'Let me taste your ware.'

Says the pie-man to Simple Simon,
'Show me first your penny.'
Says Simple Simon to the pie-man,
'Indeed I have not any!'

Nottingham Goose
Fair begins in
England 1540

1400

1500

1600

There were prizes to win on the side-shows and there were presents to take home for the family. Gifts to take home from the fair were known as 'fairings'. A popular fairing was a coloured ribbon.

O dear, what can the matter be?

O dear, what can the matter be?
Dear, dear, what can the matter be?
O dear, what can the matter be?
Johnny's so long at the fair.

He promised to buy me a pair of sleeve buttons,
A pair of new garters that cost just tuppence,
He promised to bring me a bunch of blue ribbons
To tie up my bonny brown hair.

Thames Frost Fair
1608

Great Thames
Frost Fair
1684

1700

11

1800

Victorian fairs

At the Victorian fairs in the 1800s there were . . .

- puppet plays
- pantomimes
- moving waxworks
- mermaids
- boxing and wrestling matches
- bearded ladies
- magicians
- boys and girls who danced on tight-ropes
- food to make you smack your lips.

Fun-fairs

From the 1820s railways crossed the country. Food and clothes were rushed around on rails. Now there was no need for trading fairs at all. Trains brought almost everything.

But trains could not bring FUN. So a new kind of fair began — the fun-fair.

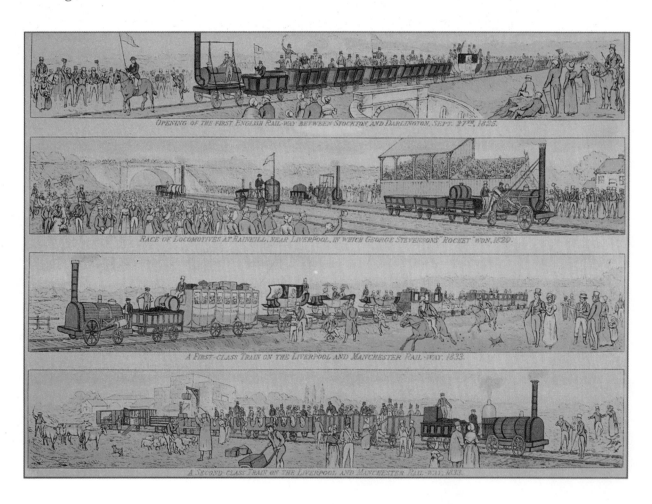

OPENING OF THE FIRST ENGLISH RAIL-WAY BETWEEN STOCKTON AND DARLINGTON, SEPT. 27TH 1825.

RACE OF LOCOMOTIVES AT RAINHILL, NEAR LIVERPOOL, IN WHICH GEORGE STEVENSONS' ROCKET WON, 1829.

A FIRST-CLASS TRAIN ON THE LIVERPOOL AND MANCHESTER RAIL-WAY, 1833.

A SECOND-CLASS TRAIN ON THE LIVERPOOL AND MANCHESTER RAIL-WAY, 1833.

Steam trains
invented
1815

1800   1810   1820   1830   1840

Steam powered rides

In Aylsham town in Norfolk, England, a man started to give rides on a new machine. It was a roundabout which had a steam engine.

The first steam-powered rides were roundabouts with wooden horses. The rides were called 'gallopers'. Later ones were steam yachts and zigzag railways called 'switchbacks'.

At the first fun-fairs there were swings and flying chairs, and stalls with hoop-la and rifle shooting.

St Bartholemew's
Fair stopped
1855

First steam
powered
roundabout 1865

First fairground
organs in Europe
1875

1850   1860   1870   1880

Some cities welcomed the new fun-fairs.

Newcastle people were worried about the money wasted at the Newcastle Horse Races each year. They set up a fair for all the family on the Town Moor. The fair was known as 'The Hoppings'.

It began in 1882 with children's races, brass band contests, football and cricket. The most popular thing was the amusement park with roundabouts and 'high fliers'.

In 1906 the first helter skelter came to The Hoppings.

Now Newcastle Hoppings is one of the biggest travelling fairs in the world. It still has helter skelters.

Did you know...

one Newcastle Hoppings stall was called 'Fire away at the milky ones'. It was a coconut shy.

The Hoppings starts in Newcastle 1882

First moving picture show at fairs 1895

First electric lights used on roundabouts 1897

1880

1890

1900

Travelling fun-fairs

Before the 1850s show-people pulled fairground rides around the country with horses. Then they began using huge steam waggons.

By the 1920s they were using lorries.

Did you know...

in 1913 George Wombwell took wild animal shows to fairs. One of his caravans wasn't pulled by a steam wagon or a lorry. It was pulled by an elephant!

Electric powered rides

New electric rides began to take the place of the old steam rides.

The show-people had their own machines to make electricity; they were called 'generators'. Electricity meant new thrills: ghost trains and waltzers, big wheels and big dippers.

There was a new food too. Candy floss machines were invented in America in the 1920s.

Did you know . . .

Dodgem cars were invented in 1927. Not many people owned cars in the 1920s. It was new and exciting to ride in a car. Dodgems are still popular today.

Amusement parks

Soon the greatest, most exciting rides were just too large to travel round the country. Some fair grounds stayed in just one place.

By the 1950s many families owned a car. The fairs didn't have to travel to the people. The people could travel to the fairs.

There were seaside fair grounds, even indoor fairs. Now we think of 'fairs' as 'fun-fairs'. They are growing bigger and bigger.

Some fun-fairs still travel around. English travelling fairs start every 14th February in King's Lynn.

Candy floss is invented 1920s

Dodgems are invented 1927

SKITTLES & COCONUTS →

Fairs today

In ancient times traders travelled around the world to go to the fairs.

Today people still travel across the world to see the biggest fairs. They don't travel the old roads by horse and camel. They fly in jets to see huge new fairs called theme parks.

Disneyland opened in California in 1955. Twenty-five years later Alton Towers opened in England. Germany has Phantasialand and France has Disneyland Paris. Fun-fairs have changed. The rides are faster and bigger and more daring.

But fairs still bring thrills and colour and magic …

they still bring fun and noise …

… and they still bring exciting food.

Now the food is chips and burgers, hot dogs and ice-cream.

Disneyland opens 1955

The 20th Century

Walt Disney World opens 1971

1950

1960

1970

Did you know...

the most popular rides at fairgrounds now are roller coasters.

© Disney
Disneyland Paris

Drayton Manor Park has the first roller coaster in Europe on which passengers ride standing up.

The world's longest roller coaster is at Lightwater Valley – it is called 'The Ultimate' and it is about two and a half kilometres long.

1980

Alton Towers
amusement Park
opens 1980

1990

Disneyland Paris
opens 1992

23

Index